Leif Eriksson

Michael Burgan

Heinemann Library
Chicago, Illinois

Design by Wilkinson Design
Maps by Kimberly Saar
Printed and bound in the U.S.A. by Lake Book Manufacturing, Inc.

06 05 04
10 9 8 7 6 5 4 3 2

Library of Congress Cataloging-in-Publication Data
Burgan, Michael.
   Leif Eriksson / Michael Burgan.
     p. cm. -- (Groundbreakers)
   Includes bibliographical references and index.
   Summary: Presents an account of the life and explorations of Leif
Eriksson, who led a group of Vikings from Greenland on a voyage which
ended on the shores of North America.
   ISBN 1-58810-596-2
   1. Leiv Eiriksson, d. ca. 1020--Juvenile literature. 2.
Explorers--America--Biography--Juvenile literature. 3.
Explorers--Scandinavia--Biography--Juvenile literature. 4.
America--Discovery and exploration--Norse--Juvenile literature. 5.
Vikings--Juvenile literature. [1. Ericson, Leif, d. ca. 1020. 2
Explorers. 3. Vikings. 4. America--Discovery and exploration--Norse.]
I. Title. II. Series.
   E105.L47 B87 2002
   970.01'3'092--dc21

2001005657

Acknowledgments
The author and publishers are grateful to the following for permission to reproduce copyright material:
pp. 4, 16, 23 The Granger Collection, New York; pp. 5, 22, 36 Wolfgang Kaehler/Corbis; pp. 6, 9, 30, 31 North Wind Picture Archives; pp. 7, 19, 21, 24, 32, 34 Courtesy of Greenland Tourism; p. 10 Gianni Dagli Orti/Corbis; p. 11 Werner Forman Archive/Viking Ship Museum, Bygdoy; p. 13 Galen Rowell/Corbis; pp. 14, 20 Werner Forman Archive/Statens Historiska Museet, Stockholm; p. 15 Macduff Everton/Corbis; pp. 17, 38 Bettmann/Corbis; p. 18 The Newberry Library, Chicago ; p. 25 Richard Olsenius/Black Star Publishing/PictureQuest; pp. 26, 28 C. M. Dixon; p. 27 Collection of the Newfoundland Museum; p. 29 Corbis; p. 33 National Museum of Denmark; p. 35 Greenland National Museum and Archives; p. 37 CP, Andrew Vaughn/AP Photo; p. 39 Main State Museum, Augusta, Maine; p. 40 Eye Ubiquitous/Corbis; p. 41 Reuters NewMedia Inc./Corbis

Cover photograph courtesy of Hulton/Archive by Getty Images

Note to the reader: Over the years, artists have depicted Vikings in ways that historians now know are not accurate. For example, Leif Eriksson and other Vikings are often shown wearing winged helmets, although we now know this to be incorrect.

Some words are shown in bold, **like this.** You can find out what they mean by looking in the glossary.

Contents

Some time around the year 1000, a **Viking knorr** pulled into a quiet harbor. On board the wooden ship, Leif Eriksson commanded a crew of 35 men. He had sailed west from Greenland, looking for new lands. He found the main part of what is now called North America, becoming the first European to set foot on that continent. He called this territory "Vinland."

Students once learned that Christopher Columbus discovered the **"New World"** of North America. Europeans ignored the Native Americans who had walked or sailed to the continent from Asia, thousands of years earlier. Columbus, however, did play an important role in world history. His voyages opened the **Western Hemisphere** to European exploration. But why was Leif's earlier voyage of discovery ignored for centuries?

Uncertain history

Unlike Columbus, Leif did not keep a diary of his journey, and the small outpost he built did not survive. For generations, the only knowledge of Leif and his travels came from stories told in Iceland. These **sagas** were originally spoken tales that were passed on from one generation to the next. The sagas were not written down until hundreds of years after Leif lived. Sometimes, the sagas were not accurate in recording historical facts.

Leif Eriksson sailed on a ship similar to this one. A typical knorr could carry up to 20 tons (18 metric tons) of cargo over long distances.

L'Anse aux Meadows is the name of the spot in Newfoundland where archeologists uncovered Norse remains.

No one in Europe knew about the sagas and their tales of Viking exploration until scholars in **Scandinavia** discovered them in the early 1600s. Eventually, the scholars realized that the sagas might describe a Viking settlement in North America that existed long before Columbus sailed west.

Proof of Leif's trip

By the 20th century, however, some scholars began to doubt that Leif and his crew had reached North America. No one had ever found proof of their trip. In other places where Vikings once lived, such as Greenland, **archeologists** had unearthed buildings and items from everyday **Norse** life. Finally, in the early 1960s, two archaeologists found what had been a small Norse village in Newfoundland, Canada. The sagas— or at least some of them—were true. Leif Eriksson had reached North America.

We have few details about Leif and the Vinland **expeditions.** But we do know some things about this great explorer, and even more about the world that shaped him.

VIKINGS, NORSEMEN, AND NORMANS

The term "Viking" is often used to describe the people from Scandinavia who thrived from about 750 to 1050. This era is sometimes called the Viking Age. "Viking" was originally the name for the raiders from Scandinavia who attacked other parts of Europe. Now, many people use the word to describe anyone from that region during the Viking Age. Leif is more accurately called a Norse or Norseman—the **descendant** of someone who came from Norway and settled on Iceland. Some Norwegians also settled in France, and their descendants are called **Normans.** They continued to play an important role in Western Europe and England after the Viking Age.

Who Was Leif Eriksson?

The **Norse** in Leif's time did not keep written records of births and deaths. No one knows for sure where or when Leif was born. He might have been born in Iceland, or perhaps on board a ship bound for Greenland. By one estimate, Leif could have been about 20 years old when he left on his first **expedition** to the west. That would make his birthdate sometime around 980. Leif probably died some time before 1025.

As a Norseman, Leif came from a people with a long **nautical** tradition. He was an expert sailor. Leif was also a respected leader among the people on Greenland. According to the **sagas,** Leif was tall, strong, handsome, and wise, "as well as being a man of moderation in all things."

"Leif the Lucky"

On one voyage, Leif saved some sailors who had survived a shipwreck. The men were fortunate that Leif had found them. He took them back to Greenland and found places for them to stay through the long winter. After his kind and heroic deed, Leif was known as "Leif the Lucky," for the good luck he brought to the stranded sailors.

Since no painting of Leif exists from his time, modern artists have painted their own ideas of what he looked like. Many details are probably not accurate.

In Greenland, Leif and his family lived on this site. The family farm was called Brattahlid ("steep hillside").

A family of adventurers

As an explorer, Leif was more than lucky. His personal courage and knowledge of the sea had deep family roots. His father Erik had been a sailor, traveling from his native Norway to Iceland. Later, Erik led the first Norse settlement on Greenland. Leif's brothers and sister also had a thirst for adventure. After Leif's return from Vinland, they made their own trips to North America. In many ways, Leif and his family were typical **Vikings,** eager to travel and find new lands where they could farm and trade.

VIKING NAMES

Family members in Viking society did not have the same last names. People took their father's first name and then added "son" or "dottir" (daughter) to it. Leif's father was Erik Thorvaldsson (son of Thorvald). Leif's sister Freydis had the last name Eriksdottir. And Leif's son was known as Thorkel Leifsson.

The World of the Vikings

In 793, **monks** on Lindisfarne, an island off England's northeast coast, saw strange ships reach their shore. On board were raiders from northern lands—**Vikings.** The Vikings stole valuables from the monks and killed anyone who resisted them. Over the next two centuries, Vikings from Norway and Denmark carried out similar raids throughout the British Isles and Europe. Swedish Vikings headed east, conquering native people in Russia, then traveling south to the ancient empire of **Byzantium.**

The brutality of Viking raids led some people to call them "the curse of the north." But at home in **Scandinavia,** most of the people were farmers who lived simple lives. The Viking raiders did not sweep through Europe because they were especially cruel or bloodthirsty. Changing conditions in Scandinavia in the 8th century sparked the raids.

A search for power

The first Vikings did not have central leaders. The Scandinavians lived in small communities ruled by chieftains. By the 700s, the number of chieftains was rising, and they competed against each other to attract more followers. Having more people loyal to them gave the chieftains more power. To prove their

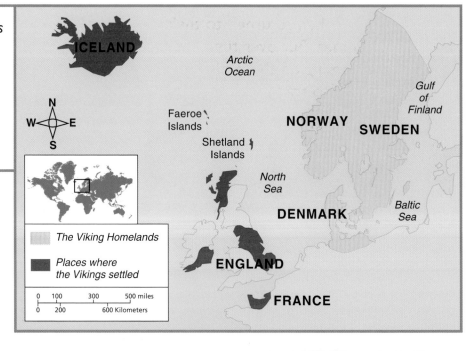

This map shows the Viking homeland of Scandinavia and some of the lands they settled.

ICELAND

Arctic Ocean

Gulf of Finland

Faeroe Islands

NORWAY

SWEDEN

Shetland Islands

N
W — E
S

North Sea

DENMARK

Baltic Sea

ENGLAND

FRANCE

The Viking Homelands

Places where the Vikings settled

0   100   300   500 miles
0   200   600 Kilometers

leadership and earn that loyalty, the chieftains needed wealth. As it became harder to find riches locally, the chieftains looked toward foreign lands as new sources of wealth.

At this time, Christian **monasteries** played an important role in Europe. They were centers of learning as well as religion. The monasteries were also wealthy. They owned beautiful items made of gold and silver, paid for by donations from faithful Christians. The Vikings knew about the monks' riches, and they knew that the monasteries did not have strong defenses. The chieftains had easy targets for their raids.

From raiders to settlers

At first, Vikings sailed in, took what they wanted, and then returned to their Scandinavian homes. But over time, many Vikings began settling on the lands they raided. They also started to trade with the local people, instead of robbing and killing them. Danish Vikings settled along the east coast of Britain and Ireland. Norwegian Vikings made their homes on the islands north of Britain, including the Orkney, Shetland, and Faeroe Islands. A rising population at home meant that farmland was becoming scarce. These new lands gave Scandinavians plenty of room of their own.

In a monk's words:

"The number of ships grows. Vikings in an endless stream, never ceasing, indeed growing. Everywhere the Christians are victims of massacres, pillaging and plundering. The Vikings conquer all in their path, and no one resists them."

Lords of the Sea

The **knorr** that Leif Eriksson sailed toward Vinland was a sturdy cargo ship. Similar boats had carried his father and other settlers to Greenland. But when the **Vikings** made their raids on Europe, they sailed sleek vessels called **longships.** Unlike the knorr, the longship was built for war. This Viking vessel developed from a boat-building tradition in **Scandinavia** that was centuries old.

Best ships of the era

The earliest Viking ships were made out of planks of soft, light wood. Later, boatbuilders used stronger oak for a ship's main body—the **keel**—and pine for the decks. Before their raids on Europe, the Vikings improved the basic design of their ships. They made the keels longer so they could sail smoothly in deeper seas. They also attached a large sail made of wool to a strong mast in the center of the ship, for added speed.

The Bayeux **Tapestry,** woven by **Normans** in the 11th century, shows how Vikings cut down trees to build their ships.

By the end of the 8th century, the Viking ships were the best in northern Europe. Light and fast, they could sail almost anywhere. The biggest were more than 118 feet (36 meters) long and carried about 100 men. The warriors used oars to steer the ship into port. When the raid ended, the Vikings made a quick escape. The ships also helped frighten their enemies. On the **prows** of some of the ships, the boatbuilders carved fierce dragon heads. The Viking warships were also known as dragon ships.

The Oseberg burial ship was probably used on rivers or close to shore. A reconstruction of the ship shows a serpent on the prow.

Traveling the seas

The Vikings did not have complex tools to help them **navigate** as they sailed. Whenever possible, they sailed within sight of land, so they could follow familiar landmarks along their route. On open seas, the Vikings relied on the positions of the Sun and stars to help guide them, and entire islands sometimes served as landmarks for longer routes.

The longships seemed to have one feature that other ships of the time lacked. On the right side, toward the rear of the ship, was an oar or rudder called a *styri* that was used for steering. This Scandinavian word led to the English word for the right side of any ship—starboard.

Their seafaring life was not always easy, but the Vikings welcomed the riches they brought home on their raids. And for adventurous **Norse** sailors such as Leif, the sea was a road to new lands.

UNCOVERING VIKING SHIPS

Most knowledge of Viking ships comes from the remains of several ships found in Scandinavia. Some of these ships were burial ships. Vikings were sometimes buried at sea in their ships, along with other items they owned during their lives. The oldest true Viking ship ever found dates from around 815 and was uncovered at Oseberg, Norway.

On to New Lands

From their settlements in Great Britain and their homes in **Scandinavia,** the **Vikings** continued to look for new lands. They called this quest *landnam*—"land-taking." One place they settled was the island of Iceland. Leif Eriksson and his family would later have a strong influence on the island's culture and history.

First settlements

The first **Norse** arrived in Iceland about 870 to find that only the areas near the ocean were suitable for farms and homes. Most of Iceland is covered with deserts, mountains, volcanoes, natural hot springs, and **glaciers.** Although the Vikings found clues that Irish **monks** had visited Iceland, they were the first people to settle there permanently.

Iceland, located about 600 miles (965 kilometers) west of Norway, is the westernmost independent state in Europe. It is about the size of Kentucky.

Several explorers are credited with discovering Iceland, including Naddod the Viking and a Norwegian named Flóki Vilgerdarson. After seeing icebergs off the coast, Flóki named it *Ísland*—"Ice land."

The **sagas** say that two Norsemen, Ingolf Arnarson and Leif Hrodmarsson, brought people and animals to Iceland for a permanent *landnam*. They and other settlers soon re-created the life they had lived in Scandinavia. They found meadows where their sheep could graze, and they grew barley. The climate in 10th-century Iceland was warmer than it is today, so more of the land could be used for farming. The sea provided plenty of fish, and the forests provided firewood.

An independent land

Word about Iceland spread to other Viking settlements, and others soon flocked to the island. The settlers came from all over, but most Icelanders were from Norway. "Norse" is used to describe the culture that developed on Iceland, which Leif and his family took with them to Greenland and Vinland.

By about 930, the Norse had settled all the available land in Iceland. Many of the newcomers had come to escape political troubles in Norway. The king, Harald, was taking away rights from the people and demanding higher taxes. In Iceland, the Norse found a freedom they thought was slipping away at home.

The Icelanders set up their own government and made their own laws. Leaders were elected to represent them at an assembly called the **Althing,** which has been compared to a modern democracy. In truth, a small group of wealthy men controlled the government. Still, a typical farmer had more independence in Iceland than he had enjoyed in Norway.

Erik the Red, Leif's father, might have lived in a longhouse like this while on Iceland. With wood in short supply, the Icelanders made use of stones and turf to help build many of their homes.

Norse Religion and Culture

Along with their farming lifestyle, the **Norse** brought their religion with them to Iceland. The people of **Scandinavia** at this time worshipped many gods. They also told stories of giants who battled the gods, and of dwarfs who lived underground. The Norse religion thrived on Iceland until about 1000, when Christianity arrived on the island.

The most important Norse god was Odin, the god of war and wisdom. Other key gods were Frey and his sister Freya, gods who ensured fertile lands and healthy children. The Norse also had high respect for Thor, who controlled the weather. The gods, the Norse believed, lived in the center of the world in a place called Asgard. Humans went to a place called Valhalla when they died. People were buried with items they might need in their life after death at Valhalla, such as tools or jewelry.

Magical writings

The Norse believed that Odin gave them a system of writing called **runes.** These were similar to letters used in the Latin alphabet, which was the most common writing system in Western Europe at the time. The Norse usually carved the runes into stones. The stones were often left out in the open, where many people could read them. Sometimes the runes carried religious messages. They often described military victories of great warriors or told about trading trips.

*Despite their image as fierce warriors, the **Vikings** were also skilled craftspeople. Many pieces of jewelry and art showed images from Norse myths, such as this pin of a serpent.*

The sagas

The massive carved runestones were impressive monuments to great people and historic events. But they were not convenient for writing letters or recording the details of history. As the Norse came into contact with Christianity, they began writing down their poems, stories, and history, and Iceland was the center of this activity. Historians have learned about the Norse in Leif's time and after from books called **sagas.**

The first sagas appeared around 1200. They tell how settlers from Norway came to Iceland. Then they trace the growth of life on the island. The language that developed on Iceland has changed very little in 1,000 years, so modern Icelanders would have no trouble reading the sagas.

The sagas are colorful stories of outlaws and heroes. They discuss the lives of kings and show details of everyday life. But the sagas are tales as well as history—not everything in them is accurate. Still, they give modern readers a taste of what Norse life was like. And the pages of the sagas introduce the adventures of Erik the Red, Leif's father and the founder of Greenland.

The Norse used 16 runes in their early writings. The first six characters stood for the sounds f, u, th, a, r, and k, so the alphabet is today called the **futhark.** The runes were made from simple, straight lines, making them easier to carve into stones.

This runestone stands outside a church in Soderkoping, Sweden. A rune could be part of a word or stand alone. The rune for "f," for example, meant "wealth."

Leif's Family and the Sagas

YOU CAN FOLLOW ERIK THE RED'S JOURNEY ON THE MAP ON P. 42.

Two **sagas** tell the story of Leif and his family. *Erik the Red's Saga* outlines the travels of Leif's father. Erik's settlement of Greenland led the way for Leif's voyage to North America. The *Greenlanders' Saga*, a shorter tale, also recounts the lives of the father and son who took **Norse** culture to new lands. Together, the two sagas are sometimes called the *Vinland Sagas*. Of the two stories, the *Greenlanders' Saga* is considered the most accurate by some historians, though parts of it are probably exaggerations.

A man on the move

Erik was the son of Thorvald Asvaldson. His nickname "the Red" came from his striking red hair and beard. He and his father lived in Jaren, Norway. Some time around 960, they had a violent argument with their neighbors, leading to murder. They were **banished** from the country and sailed to Iceland.

By this time, Norse settlers had already claimed the best farmland in Iceland. Erik ended up on a small farm with poor soil. Soon he was involved in another fight with neighbors that ended in bloodshed. He and his wife Thjodhild moved again, settling on a small island. Trouble broke out again, and in 982 Erik was convicted of another murder. The local **Althing** ordered him banished for three years.

All copies of the sagas were written by hand. Many of them were also illustrated with beautiful drawings. This is called illuminating.

At 840,000 square miles (1.35 million square kilometers), Greenland is more than twice as large as Texas and California combined and is the world's largest island. Most of the island is covered by snow and ice. When Erik arrived, he did not find any native people. At that time, these people, called **Dorset** by **archaeologists,** only lived on Greenland's northwest coast. Erik, however, did find remains from past Dorset settlements.

This modern drawing shows what life might have been like on Greenland soon after the Norse arrived. They needed to repair ships, make food, and build homes.

Erik had heard about an unsettled land west of Iceland, near small islands where men often hunted for walrus and seals. He sailed for this land and spent several years there. He returned to Iceland in 985, hoping to start his own settlement on this new land. To encourage others to join him, he gave the island an attractive name: Greenland.

Erik the leader

Many Icelanders were willing to move to an unknown land. Land and food were becoming scarce in Iceland. Erik's tale of green fields and plentiful food tempted enough Icelanders to fill 25 ships. Erik could now escape his enemies forever, claim the best farmland, and be the leader of his own small settlement.

In 986, Erik's ships left Iceland, carrying supplies and farm animals as well as people—everything the settlers needed to start a new life on Greenland. Although some ships were lost at sea and others turned back, Erik had several hundred people with him when he reached the southern coast of Greenland. He settled on a farm he called Brattahlid, which became the center of what was called the Eastern Settlement. This was followed by the slightly smaller Western Settlement, along the west coast.

Life on Greenland

On Greenland, the **sagas** say, Erik was "held in the highest esteem and everyone deferred to his authority." He continued to worship the old **Norse** gods, and he set up a government like the one on Iceland.

Erik's family on Greenland included his wife Thjodhild and four children: Leif, his brothers Thorvald and Thorstein, and their sister Freydis. Their farm was located on a beautiful grassy spot along a **fjord** later known as Eiriksfjord. Erik, his family, and the other settlers tried to raise crops, but the short growing season made farming difficult. Instead, the Greenlanders survived by raising cattle and sheep, hunting **caribou,** seal, and other animals, and by fishing in the Atlantic Ocean.

This wood carving shows a seal hunt. Greenlanders used similar boats and spears on their hunting trips.

Traders again

The animals the Greenlanders caught were important not only as food. They also provided many of the goods that the settlers traded with Iceland and Norway. Even more than on Iceland, Erik and his people needed valuable items they could not find on Greenland. These included timber, for building ships and other wooden items, and iron. In return for these and other goods, the Greenlanders traded animal furs, ivory taken from walrus tusks, and wool from their sheep. In later years, another prized item from Greenland was live polar bears. Wealthy Europeans valued them as rare gifts.

Leif the sailor

Like his father, Leif had an urge to travel, and he was an excellent sailor. Leif sailed trading ships to Norway. According to some stories, he made the first direct trip from Greenland to Scotland and then the continent of Europe, without stopping first in Iceland. In Norway, Leif was considered "one of King Olaf Tryggvason's men," as one saga says. Leif served the king and did whatever he asked.

On one trip from Greenland to Europe, Leif's ship lost its way and landed on the Hebrides Islands, near Scotland. During his stay, Leif fell in love with a local woman named Thorgunna. They had a child together, a son named Thorgils. Leif had at least one other child with a different woman, a son named Thorkel.

With his successful trading ventures and his father's important position, Leif must have lived as good a life as anyone on Greenland. Brattahlid grew over the years, as the family added more buildings, and new settlers helped the **colony** on Greenland continue to prosper. Leif, however, was ready for new adventures, and he thought about visiting another unknown land farther west of Greenland.

Many people on Greenland still live in small settlements near the coast, much like Leif and his family did more than 1,000 years ago.

Voyages West

You can follow Bjarni's and Leif's journeys on the maps on pp. 42–43.

Shortly after Erik settled in Greenland, an Icelander named Bjarni Herjolfsson returned home from Norway, where he discovered that his father had sold his farm and moved to Greenland with Erik. Determined to spend the winter with his father, Bjarni sailed west.

Bjarni's discovery

Bjarni did not know the exact route to Greenland, and bad weather made it hard for him and his crew to determine their course. A storm blew them far to the south and west. When Bjarni spotted land, he did not think it was Greenland. That island, he knew, had great mountains, but the shore in front of him had forests and small hills.

Bjarni and his crew then headed north. After sailing two more days, the crew spotted land again. This time Bjarni reasoned that they had not reached Greenland because the land in front of them did not have **glaciers.** The crew wanted to go ashore anyway, but Bjarni sailed on. They continued northward, and in three days, they came upon a third landmass. It had mountains and glaciers, but Bjarni doubted it was Greenland. He told the crew, "this land seems to offer nothing of use." Finally, after sailing southeast for four more days, the ship reached Greenland, and Bjarni was reunited with his father.

*Leif's ship may have had a weather vane similar to this one on its **prow.** Vanes were used to judge the direction of the wind and also may have played a part in **nautical** rituals.*

Tempting tales

Bjarni never sailed west again. He was criticized back in Norway for his lack of curiosity about the lands he had seen. But these western lands interested Erik and Leif.

Some time toward the end of the 10th century, Leif bought Bjarni's ship, planning an **expedition** he hoped his father would lead. Erik was no longer a young man, but he reluctantly agreed. However, as he rode to the docks to start the voyage, his horse tripped and threw him to the ground. When he got up, Erik realized his foot was injured and he could not sail. Leif then took over as commander.

*A replica of a Norse ship from Leif's era cruises the North Atlantic Ocean. Many modern shipbuilders have sailed copies of **Norse** ships.*

Helluland

Leif sailed first for the last land Bjarni had seen on his voyage to Greenland. Just as Bjarni said, it was mountainous and covered with glaciers, with no grass in sight. Leif and a few sailors rowed ashore in a small boat, took several steps, then returned to the ship. Leif said, "As far as this land is concerned it can't be said of us as of Bjarni, that we did not set foot on shore." Because of the rocky landscape, Leif called it Helluland—"Stone-slab Land." Leif had reached what is today called Baffin Island.

On to Vinland

YOU CAN FOLLOW LEIF'S JOURNEY ON THE MAP ON P. 42.

Sailing on, Leif and his crew reached a second stretch of land. It was covered in forests, with sandy beaches along the shore. Once again, Leif was the first **Norse** to set foot there. He called it Markland, meaning "Forest Land." Leif did not stay on shore long, since he was eager to reach the last of Bjarni's three discoveries.

Two days later, Leif and his crew spotted land, with an island just north of it. They sailed first to the island and found grass covered with dew. There was so much water, the sailors collected it in their hands and drank it, "and thought they had never tasted anything so sweet."

Back on the ship, Leif sailed west, heading for the mainland. Soon the ship lay motionless—it had run aground during low tide. Leif and his men were eager to explore the land, so they left the ship where it sat, instead of waiting for the tide to bring them closer to shore. Eventually, the crew towed the ship up a river and anchored it in a lake.

Exploring the land

Leif decided that this was a good place to spend the winter. The sailors built small cabins, so the site was later called Leifsbudir ("Leif's Houses"). Leif and his crew found plenty of salmon in the lake and the river, bigger than any they had caught in Greenland.

*This stretch of Labrador coastline may have been the beaches Leif spotted on Markland. In the **sagas,** the beaches are called Furdustrandir ("Wonder Strand").*

*A modern engraving shows Leif and his crew landing at Vinland. The dragon **prow** was common on **Viking** warships, but not ocean-going ships used for trade and exploration.*

Everything about this new land seemed welcoming. Leif saw that there were plenty of fields for animals to graze. He split his crew into two groups. One remained at the camp, while the other explored the region. He limited how far the men could go—they had to be able to return to the camp by nightfall.

An important discovery

One evening, a sailor named Tyrkir was late coming back to camp. Leif was preparing to send out a search party, when Tyrkir finally returned. He burst with excitement as he told Leif he had found grapevines and grapes. Grapes did not grow in Greenland, but Tyrkir recognized them from his childhood in Germany. The Norse sometimes drank wine, which had first come to them through Germany and Italy, though only the wealthy could afford it. The next day, Leif and his men began cutting grapes and vines to bring back to Greenland. Because of the grapes, Leif called this rich, new land Vinland—"Wineland."

WINE OR GRASS?

The Norse word *vin* can be said two ways. One way, it means "wine," and the other way it means "grassland." Some historians have suggested that Leif named Vinland for its grassy fields, not its grapes. Most people, however, accept the possibility that Leif could have found wild grapes or berries growing in Vinland.

23

A Safe Return, Another Voyage

The winds favored Leif's boat as it sailed back to Greenland. Nearing his homeland, Leif spotted something drifting in the water —a small boat with people on board. Leif commanded his crew to sail close to the boat, so he could see if they needed help.

The man in charge of the boat was a Norwegian named Thorir. He had heard of Erik the Red and his settlement on Greenland. Leif invited Thorir and his crew to come onto his ship, because the seas were dangerous for a small craft. Fifteen people joined Leif and sailed to Greenland. After this rescue, Leif was called "the Lucky."

Luckily, Leif did not have to sail through ice like this. "Drift ice" was not common off Greenland until about 1300.

The detailed account of Leif's exploration of Vinland comes from the *Greenlanders' Saga.* In *Erik the Red's Saga*, the story is different—and much shorter. In just a few sentences, the saga writer explains that Leif was sailing from Norway to Greenland when his ship blew off course. He then found a land with "fields of self-sown wheat and vines" and many maple trees. The saga does not mention Bjarni Herjolfsson's voyage, and Helluland and Markland appear later. These differences show how hard it has been for historians to discover the facts of the explorations.

You can follow Leif's and Thorvald's journeys on the maps on pp. 42–43.

A brother's voyage

According to the *Greenlanders' Saga*, when Leif reached Greenland, he was something of a hero: "Leif had now become very wealthy and was held in high respect." The Greenlanders listened closely as Leif and his men described what they had seen and done on their voyage. One of Leif's brothers, Thorvald, thought that Leif had not explored as much of Vinland as he could have. Leif was not ready to travel again, so he suggested that Thorvald take his ship and sail to Vinland. Thorvald agreed and began preparing for his own **expedition.**

New explorations

Sailing with a crew of 30, Thorvald reached Vinland by autumn. He stayed at Leifsbudir over the winter, with his men fishing for their food. In the spring, Thorvald sent some of his men to explore lands to the west. They took a small boat and found more forests and white beaches. Many islands dotted the shallow waters offshore.

Until this point, neither Leif nor Thorvald had seen any sign of native people. This search party, however, found a wooden trough used to hold grain. Someone must have once lived on this land—or still did.

After spending another winter at Leifsbudir, Thorvald sailed his ship eastward. A storm tossed the ship ashore and damaged its **keel.** The men repaired the ship, and Thorvald named the spot Kjalarnes ("Keel's Point"). They then continued east, exploring more of this vast region.

Forests such as this one, on Markland, held timber that would have been useful on Greenland and Iceland for building ships.

25

Meeting the "Skraeling"

Thorvald sailed Leif's ship to Markland and reached a **cove** near land covered with forests. As he went ashore, Thorvald told his crew, "This is an attractive spot, and here I would like to build my farm." This plan to settle on Markland, however, was soon threatened. For the first time, the **Norse** saw native people in the new land.

During winter months, the Norse played board games to pass the time. These markers were used for a game similar to chess.

Conflict

Returning to the ship, Thorvald spotted something in the distance—three canoes, each carried by three men. The native people were **ancestors** of either the Innu or Beothuk people. Like other peoples of the region, the Innu and Beothuk were expert hunters and fishers. The Norse called all the native people they met in Greenland and Vinland **skraeling.** This insulting term meant "ugly people" or "weaklings." Thorvald and his men did not wait to see if the skraeling were friendly. The Norse attacked and captured eight of them. The other skraeling ran off as Thorvald's men killed the eight captives. This marked the first battle ever between Europeans and natives of North America.

You can follow Thorvald's journey on the map on p. 43.

Despite this successful **skirmish,** Thorvald was uneasy. After further scouting of the area, he realized his camp was surrounded by skraeling settlements. The *Greenlanders' **Saga*** says that as the Norse slept that night, they were startled by a loud voice. "Wake up, Thorvald, and all your companions," the mysterious voice said. "Get to the ship with all your men and leave this land as quickly as you can."

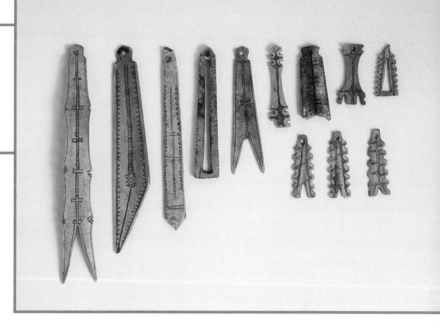

The Beothuk were skilled craftworkers who made the most of the materials available. These carved pendants are made of bone.

The skraeling's revenge

Thorvald rose to see a small fleet of canoes closing in on their campsite. He organized a defense but told his men not to fight back if possible. As the skraeling's arrows whizzed by, the Norse were able to get on their ship and escape. When they were safely away, Thorvald saw that he had been hit. He knew the wound would kill him, and he directed his crew to take him to the site he had chosen for his farm. "Perhaps the words I spoke will prove true enough and I will dwell there awhile," he said.

BEOTHUK LIFE

The Beothuk fished for salmon and hunted **caribou** and seal. To catch caribou, the people sometimes worked together, driving herds of caribou into a system of fences, trapping them so they were easier to kill. Centuries after the Norse came, the Beothuk lost access to their hunting grounds as European settlers moved in. The last known Beothuk died in 1829.

The crew did as Thorvald asked, and when he died they buried him at the farm site and marked the site with a cross. They were Christians, like most of the Norse from Greenland. The sailors then spent one more winter at Leifsbudir, gathering grapes and grapevines to bring back to Greenland. When they returned home, the saga says the crew "had plenty of news to tell Leif."

The Next Voyages

YOU CAN FOLLOW GUDRID AND KARLSEFNI'S JOURNEYS ON THE MAP ON P. 43.

The **sagas** do not say how Leif reacted to the news of his brother's death. But his other brother, Thorstein, decided it was his turn to sail to Vinland. He wanted to find Thorvald's body and bring it back to Greenland for a proper burial. Using Leif's **knorr,** Thorstein sailed with 25 men and his wife, Gudrid.

Thorstein's short trip

Both of the *Vinland Sagas* mention Thorstein's trip, though *Erik the Red's Saga* does not describe it as a mission to find Thorvald. That saga does not mention Thorvald's **expedition** at all. The sagas, agree, however, that Thorstein had a difficult time after he left Greenland, when a storm tossed the ship off course. By the end of autumn, Thorstein returned to Greenland, but he and his crew were "worn out and in poor shape."

According to the *Greenlanders' Saga*, Thorstein landed at the Western Settlement. He found housing for his crew, and he and

his wife stayed with a local farmer. That winter, an illness swept through the settlement, killing many people—including Thorstein. In the spring, Gudrid took her husband's body back to Brattahlid. She buried him there and moved in with her brother-in-law. Leif, content to stay in Greenland, did not plan another trip to locate Thorvald's body.

*Thorstein's and Thorvald's graves may have been marked with crosses such as this. Unlike many other **Vikings,** they were Christians.*

28

The Innu, native people of Labrador, built homes such as this one during the time the Norse explored the waters near their land.

A large settlement

The summer that Thorstein Eriksson died, a wealthy trader named Thorfinn Karlsefni sailed to Greenland from Norway. He spent the following winter at Brattahlid with Leif and his family. During that time, Karlsefni fell in love with Gudrid. With Leif's permission, Gudrid and Karlsefni got married.

Greenlanders still talked about settling in Vinland, and Karlsefni decided to lead an expedition to set up a **colony.** Once again, Leif allowed the use of his huts at Leifsbudir, though he had no interest in making the trip. Karlsefni and Gudrid sailed with at least 65 others, including five women. The settlers brought animals and seeds, so they could recreate their farming life in their new home.

Peaceful trade

The settlers had an easy trip to Vinland, and they quickly settled in at Leif's camp. For almost a year, the **Norse** lived on their own, but during their second summer, some **skraeling** came out of the woods to investigate the livestock Karlsefni had brought. This first encounter could have ended with bloodshed, as Thorvald's had. The native people were frightened by Karlsefni's bull, and they could not understand the foreigners' language. Somehow the two groups managed to communicate, and the skraeling tried to trade for weapons. Karlsefni said no, but the Norse did trade milk for some of the skraeling's furs.

Last Vinland Adventures

You can follow Gudrid and Karlsefni's journeys on the map on p. 43.

According to *Erik the Red's Saga,* Karlsefni and his people set up camps at two new locations, Straumfjord and Hóp. This saga also records peaceful trade between the natives and the **Norse.** But both books also describe bloody clashes between the two sides. In the *Greenlanders' Saga*, a year passed after the first round of trading with the **skraeling.** When they returned, they tried again to trade for weapons. One of Karlsefni's servants killed a skraeling who tried to steal weapons. The Norse expected more violence to follow.

A violent end

Karlsefni prepared a small force to meet the skraeling at a nearby field. When they fought, "a large number of natives were killed." Despite this victory, Karlsefni was uneasy about staying in Vinland. The land was rich with game and offered much better farming than Greenland, but the Norse knew they would never be safe from skraeling attacks. The settlers spent one more winter in Vinland, then prepared to return home. Just as Leif and Thorvald had done, Karlsefni loaded his ship with grapevines and animal skins and sailed back to Greenland.

*Although this scene of **Viking** warriors is not from Vinland, it shows typical Norse weapons of the era. The battle-axe, lower center, was especially popular.*

Freydis wanted to make sure that the witnesses of her brutal murders would not tell anyone about her crime. However, the story was later told in the sagas.

A modern illustration shows Freydis after her bloody deed. Leif and Freydis had the same father—Erik the Red— but different mothers.

Freydis the murderer

The last member of Leif's family to travel to Vinland was his sister Freydis. Of all the trips described in the *Vinland Sagas*, some historians think that Freydis's story is the least likely to be completely true. Once again, the sagas disagree on the details. The *Greenlanders' Saga* says she led her own **expedition,** after receiving Leif's permission to use his buildings at Leifsbudir. However, *Erik the Red's Saga* mentions her as a passenger on the trip led by Thorfinn Karlsefni.

In *Erik the Red's Saga*, Freydis bravely defends herself when she is attacked by skraeling. But her most shameful act, as described in the *Greenlanders' Saga*, followed an argument between Freydis and other settlers on Vinland. The problem began when Freydis reached Leifsbudir and found that two men had already moved in to the houses. After an argument, the men left, but they and Freydis continued to have disagreements.

That winter, Freydis convinced her husband to kill her two rivals and their supporters, then she cold-heartedly murdered five women. Back in Greenland, Leif found out about the murders. Although angered by his sister's behavior, he did not punish her. He decided to leave that to God.

31

Leif in Greenland

The *Vinland **Sagas*** end with Karlsefni's safe return to Greenland. From there, he and his family ended up in Iceland. The sagas do not mention what happened to Leif's family or if other **Norse** ever sailed again to Vinland. Leif, however, probably served as one of the leaders of Greenland until his death. There is no written record of when this occurred. By 1025, however, Leif's son Thorkel was the chieftain at Eiriksfjord, which means that Leif was probably dead by then.

A small wooden church sits near the site where "Thjodhild's church" was found in 1961. Buried near the foundation of the old church were the bones of about 100 Norse men, women, and children.

A new faith

Along with finding new lands for the Norse to explore, Leif is credited with bringing Christianity to Greenland. *Erik the Red's Saga* describes how Olaf Tyrggvason, the king of Norway, asked Leif to convert the Greenlanders to this religion. Leif was doubtful, because he knew many people—including his father—were devoted to the traditional Norse gods. Still, Leif agreed to do what the king asked.

It was on the voyage back to Greenland from Norway, the saga says, that Leif discovered Vinland and rescued the stranded sailors. (This version of Leif's discovery disagrees with the story in the *Greenlanders' Saga*, described on pages 21-24.) When he returned home, Leif introduced the teachings of Christianity, "telling [the Norse] how excellent and glorious this faith was." This took place, some sources say, about 1000.

Christians in Greenland followed the teachings of the **Roman Catholic Church.** The first **bishop** was assigned to the island around 1124, but there is no proof that he actually reached Greenland. When a bishop finally reached the island in the 13th century, he settled at Gardar, Greenland's largest farm. His church there was the most important on the island.

As Leif expected, some people did not accept the new religion. His mother Thjodhild, however, eagerly embraced it. She ordered a church to be built not far from Brattahlid, and Leif and the rest of his family also seemed to have become Christians.

A challenge to the sagas

Despite the story of Leif's importance to religion in Greenland, most historians doubt it is true. Some scholars think the Greenlanders might have converted to Christianity before they reached the island. Others say the conversion came later in the 11th century.

In either case, there is evidence of an early Christian church on Greenland. In 1961, construction workers found the remains of a simple church not far from where Brattahlid stood. **Archaeologists** have determined that the church was built around 1000. Like the Norse homes, the church was made out of wood and turf. Some people have suggested this was Thjodhild's church, built with Erik's permission, even though he still worshipped the old gods.

The cross is the most important symbol in Christianity. This cross, made of ivory from Greenland, was used by a Danish princess.

Shortly after Leif's death, the **Viking** Age came to an end. Most historians place the end of the Viking Age at about 1050. For others, 1066 marks the end of that era. That year, the **Normans** of France invaded England and took control of the country. By then, the Vikings and their **descendants** were no longer seen as bloodthirsty outsiders. In politics, economics, and religion, they were part of the larger Western European culture.

Greenland after Leif

Although the voyages to Vinland ended around 1020, life went on in Greenland. Immigrants from Iceland and Europe and the birth of new children helped raise the island's population. By 1100, Greenland had an estimated 1,000 citizens, and the number peaked in about 1300 with more than 2,000. Still, this population was tiny compared with Iceland, which had about 70,000 people.

By the middle of the 14th century, the population on Greenland began to decrease. The smaller Western Settlement disappeared completely. Around 1364, a Norwegian priest wrote, **"Skraeling** have destroyed all the Western Settlement. There is abundance of horses, goats, bulls, and sheep all wild, and no people..." Contact with Native Americans called **Inuit** may have played a role in ending the Western Settlement. But the eventual end of the **Norse** presence on Greenland had several causes.

In 1408, a wedding took place at Hvalsey Church, the remains of which are shown here. This wedding was the last documented Norse event on Greenland.

The Inuit originally lived in Alaska, then moved eastward across northern Canada. Around 1300, the Inuit reached Greenland and had their first contact with the Norse. The two peoples seemed to get along at first, but later they had violent clashes. Unlike the Norse, the Inuit adapted to the colder climate of the 14th century. Today, Inuit children read folktales about their **ancestors** and the Norse.

A 19th-century painting shows Greenland Inuit performing a ring dance, a social custom they learned from the Norse.

Climate and habits

Between the settlement of Greenland and the 14th century, the climate on Greenland changed. The temperature grew colder, and farming became more difficult. The colder temperatures, however, were not the only problem the Greenlanders faced. The Greenlanders added to the crisis by keeping old habits. The cooler weather made it hard for farmers to keep raising cattle, but they kept trying, instead of moving to the coasts and hunting for seal, as the Inuit did.

Last contact

During the first part of the 14th century, a **knorr** regularly sailed from Norway to Greenland. These trips stopped sometime around 1367. After this date, the written records mention only a few trips to the island by Europeans, usually the result of ships blown off their course during a storm. The regular voyages Leif made to Norway were a thing of the past.

According to **archaeologists,** the Norse either died off or left Greenland for good around 1450. This was confirmed in 1721, when a **Protestant missionary** came to convert the Greenlanders. All he found were Inuit. The descendants of Leif Eriksson had disappeared from history.

The Search for Vinland

As early as 1075, Europeans knew that Vinland existed, though they did not know the details of Leif's trip. A German priest named Adam of Bremen had met the king of Denmark, who told Adam about "still another island named Vinland, since there grow there wild grapes and they give the best wine."

Leif and his crew lived in houses similar to these, shown in a modern reconstruction at L'Anse aux Meadows. A small hut at the site held a shop for making iron—the first ironworks in the **New World.**

Vinland first appears in Icelandic writings toward the end of the 11th century, though once again, the sources say nothing about Leif. In one book, Leif's discovery is called "Vinland the Good," and this name also appears in later writings. Vinland, Helluland, and Markland are mentioned in several other works, but the *Vinland Sagas* remain the most detailed account of Leif, his adventurous family, and the lands they explored.

A modern quest

As scholars studied the **sagas,** they argued whether Vinland truly existed, and if it did, where it was located. By the 20th century, several scholars suggested that Vinland was in northeast Canada, and Leif might have come ashore at L'Anse aux Meadows, a small village on the northwestern tip of Newfoundland.

In 1960, a Norwegian explorer named Helge Ingstad came to L'Anse aux Meadows, searching for signs that Leif landed there. Local people took him to a meadow near a bay. A river emptied

The Snorri, *a replica ship built in Maine, sails past an island near L'Anse aux Meadows in 2000. It was part of a fleet that sailed there to mark the 1,000th anniversary of Leif's famous trip.*

into the bay, just as it is described in the sagas. Ingstad knew that Leif could have easily pulled his boat ashore at this spot. Then, about 300 feet (90 meters) from the water, Ingstad saw the remains of foundations in the ground. He realized that homes probably once sat on those foundations—homes occupied by Leif and the **Norse.** Ingstad sensed he had discovered Vinland.

Proof from the Earth

From 1961 until 1968, Ingstad and his wife, Anne Stine Ingstad, dug through the remains and the land surrounding them. They and other **archaeologists** eventually uncovered eight building sites. The largest was about 70 feet (21 meters) long and about 55 feet (17 meters) wide. It had five or six rooms. Perhaps Leif had lived here during his stay. Scattered around the house were pits where fires were built to cook food. Ingstad also found several items that the Norse used on Greenland and Iceland around the time Leif sailed. These included iron nails and a large bronze pin used to hold together a cloak.

In Helge Ingestad's words:

"There was so much here at L'Anse aux Meadows that reminded me of what I had seen of the surroundings of the Norse farms in Greenland ... Here the people from the Arctic island would have felt at home."

Scientific testing confirmed that the items came from Leif's time, and Ingstad proved his claim that he had found a Norse settlement in North America. He argued that Leif Eriksson had reached Vinland, as the sagas claimed, and L'Anse aux Meadows was one spot where Leif and other Norse had lived.

Further Exploration

Helge Ingstad's findings brought more **archaeologists** to L'Anse aux Meadows. In 1973, the Canadian government sponsored a new dig. Workers discovered a number of wooden items in a bog near the site, including a barrel top and a bark container. From all the evidence gathered, and using their knowledge of **Norse** culture, the archaeologists have a more complete view of what Leif and his sailors did in Vinland.

A base for exploration

The *Greenlanders' **Saga*** calls the main Norse camp in Vinland Leifsbudir. In *Erik the Red's Saga*, the camp is called Straumfjord. These could be two different names for the same place—the site found at L'Anse aux Meadows. Some experts, however, suggest that Straumfjord was farther south. Whatever the site was called, it was just one part of the larger region called Vinland. Leif and the Norse used the buildings there as their base camp for further explorations. At times, they returned to their camp with items to bring back to Greenland, including lumber.

Leifsbudir was a village, able to house up to 90 people. Although that number may seem small, it is almost ten percent of the entire population of Greenland at the time Leif sailed. Still, Leif was not trying to set up a permanent **colony** in Vinland, as Erik the Red had done in Greenland. Leif wanted to make money by bringing useful resources to Greenland

Helge Ingstad explains Leif's journey at a press conference announcing the discovery of Vinland.

and the rest of the **Scandinavian** world. On the trips made by his relatives and Thorfinn Karlsefni, Leif would have taken some of the profits, since he had found Vinland and served as the leader of Greenland after Erik's death.

Helge Ingstad worked hard to convince scientists and historians that he had found Norse remains in Newfoundland. Throughout his life, Ingstad was always ready for a challenge. Born in Norway in 1899, Ingstad gave up a career as a lawyer and turned to a life of research and adventure. He lived as a fur trapper in a remote part of Canada, then explored Norse ruins in Greenland before heading to Newfoundland and Leif's settlement. Ingstad died in 2001.

An important nut

The archaeologists found an important piece of evidence that showed that the Norse sailed far beyond their camp at Leifsbudir. Scattered at the site were butternut shells. Similar to walnuts, butternuts cannot grow in Newfoundland. The climate would have been too cold for them even during the warmer years of the 11th century. They may have come from sites further south, along with the grapes Leif found.

Other artifacts

So far, L'Anse aux Meadows is the only site in North America where historians are fairly certain that Leif worked and stayed. Some people have claimed to have found Norse **artifacts** elsewhere, but only one is genuine. A penny found on the coast of Maine was made in Norway a few decades after Leif died. The penny could have been brought to the site by Native Americans, who might have gotten it by trading with other tribes or directly with the Norse.

The "Maine Penny" was first uncovered in 1957 and was thought to be from 12th-century England. Further researched proved its Norse origins.

Leif's Legacy

Why are historians and others fascinated by Leif Eriksson and his travels? In part, because for so long they knew so little about him and the mysterious Vinland. What scholars did know came from books that might have been more like folk tales than history. Instead, modern science has shown that much in the **sagas** is true.

Leif also fascinates because of what he did. He set foot on a continent that Europeans never knew existed—and that most would not learn about for almost 500 years. His relatives made the first contact with the Native Americans of North America. Unfortunately, in a pattern repeated hundreds of years later, this relationship turned violent.

The Viking legacy

The discovery of Vinland was part of a long process of westward movement. Leif reflected the best values of the **Vikings** before him, who sought new places where they could farm and trade. Leif had their bravery and curiosity about distant lands—without, apparently, their thirst for violence.

Leif was also part of a distinct **Norse** culture that developed on Iceland and Greenland. For a brief time, that culture existed in Vinland as well. But the Norse's short stay there meant that their culture would not leave a lasting mark, as it did elsewhere.

This statue of Leif Eriksson stands in Reykjavik, Iceland, and bears the words, "Son of Iceland, Discoverer of Vinland." The statue was a gift from the United States government.

Tourists visiting Leif's camp at L'Anse aux Meadows meet actors playing Norse settlers from the 11th century. The actors explain how the Norse lived in Vinland.

Questions remain

Although the work at L'Anse aux Meadows has answered many questions about Leif Eriksson and Vinland, some things are still unclear. Until other Norse sites are found, **archaeologists** will not know for sure where Leif traveled after he built Leifsbudir. The real reason why the Norse stopped sailing to Vinland is also open. The presence of the **skraeling,** as described in the sagas, played a part. Perhaps the Norse also realized it was not worth making the long trip to Vinland for lumber or other goods. They could get wood by sailing to Markland, which they seemed to do even after they stopped visiting Vinland, and grapes were readily available through European trade.

Scientists and historians will continue to search for signs of Leif and the Norse in North America. What they learn should help fill in the gaps about this great explorer and his times.

A FASCINATING FAKE

In 1898, a Minnesota farmer found what he claimed was a Norse runestone. The **runes** described a trip made in 1354 from Vinland to what is now the United States. At first some experts claimed that the stone was a modern creation. Then, years later, some people argued that the stone was real, and proof that the Norse had reached Minnesota. Today, the "Kensington Stone" is once again considered a fake.

41

Maps

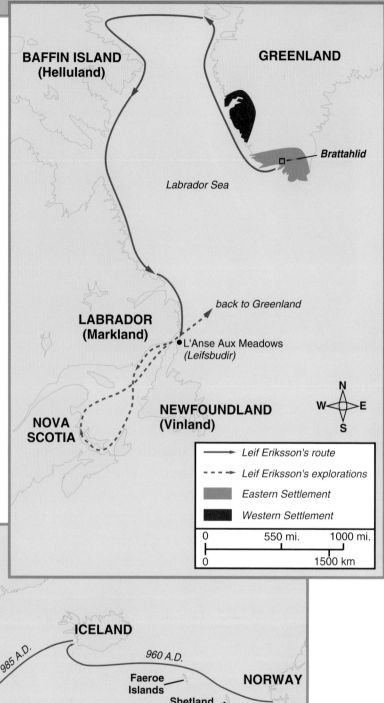

BAFFIN ISLAND
(Helluland)

GREENLAND

Brattahlid

Labrador Sea

LABRADOR
(Markland)

back to Greenland

L'Anse Aux Meadows
(Leifsbudir)

NEWFOUNDLAND
(Vinland)

NOVA
SCOTIA

N
W   E
S

	Leif Eriksson's route
	Leif Eriksson's explorations
	Eastern Settlement
	Western Settlement

0   550 mi.   1000 mi.

0   1500 km

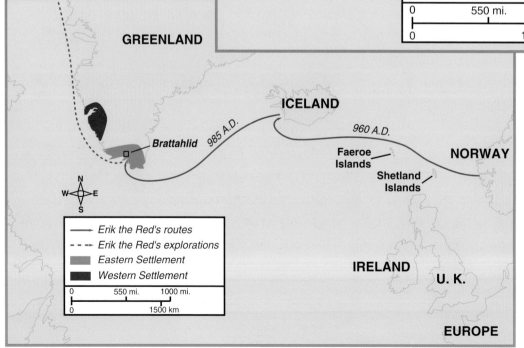

GREENLAND

ICELAND

985 A.D.   960 A.D.

Brattahlid

NORWAY

Faeroe
Islands

Shetland
Islands

N
W   E
S

	Erik the Red's routes
	Erik the Red's explorations
	Eastern Settlement
	Western Settlement

0   550 mi.   1000 mi.

0   1500 km

IRELAND

U. K.

EUROPE

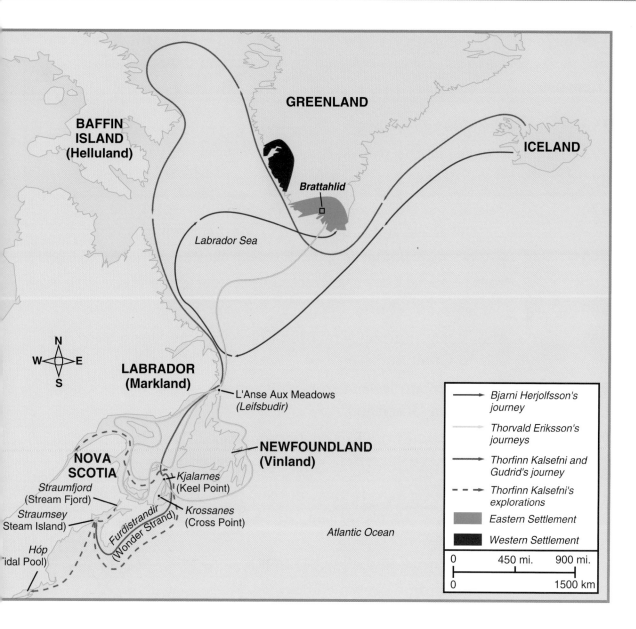

GREENLAND

BAFFIN ISLAND (Helluland)

ICELAND

Brattahlid

Labrador Sea

N
W — E
S

LABRADOR (Markland)

L'Anse Aux Meadows (*Leifsbudir*)

NEWFOUNDLAND (Vinland)

NOVA SCOTIA
Straumfjord (Stream Fjord)
Straumsey Steam Island)
Kjalarnes (Keel Point)
Krossanes (Cross Point)
Furdistrandir (Wonder Strand)
Hóp idal Pool)

Atlantic Ocean

→	Bjarni Herjolfsson's journey
→	Thorvald Eriksson's journeys
→	Thorfinn Kalsefni and Gudrid's journey
- - →	Thorfinn Kalsefni's explorations
▨	Eastern Settlement
▮	Western Settlement

0 ———— 450 mi. ———— 900 mi.
0 ———————————— 1500 km

Historians have disagreed for years about Leif's journeys and those of the other **Vikings** who landed in North America. They have used the descriptions in the **sagas** to try to find out where the **Norse** may have landed, and they have used knowledge of ocean currents to reconstruct the sea voyages. However, the sagas may not be completely true, and ocean currents may have changed. The routes shown here are based on the facts we have, but they are still estimates.

Timeline

> **Note:** Some of these dates are not exact. There is a lot that the Vikings did not write down, and historians disagree on when some things actually happened.

750	The **Viking** Age begins.
793	Vikings raid the **monastery** at Lindisfarne, England.
870	The first **Norse** settlers reach Iceland.
930	Iceland's general assembly, the **Althing,** meets for the first time. It is still active and is the world's oldest surviving parliament.
960	Erik the Red and his father, Thorvald Asvaldson, are **banished** from Norway. They sail to Iceland to start a new life.
980	Leif Eriksson is born.
982	After being accused of murder, Erik is banished from Iceland. He sails to Greenland.
985	Erik returns to Iceland to recruit settlers to join him at a new **colony** on Greenland.
986	Erik establishes the Eastern Settlement on Greenland.
	Bjarni Herjolfsson sights land west of Greenland.
1000	Leif sails westward from Greenland and explores Helluland, Markland, and Vinland. The Norse build a base camp at L'Anse aux Meadows.
	Leif rescues stranded sailors off the coast of Greenland and earns the name "Leif the Lucky."
	One source says Leif introduces Christianity to Greenland.
1000-1015	Other Norse **expeditions,** led by Thorvald Eriksson, Freydis Eriksdottir, and Thorfinn Karlsefni, explore Vinland.
	The first contact between Native Americans of North America and Europeans is made.
1025	Leif's son Thorkel is chieftain at Eiriksfjord, meaning that Leif probably died some time before this.
1066	The **Norman** invasion of England marks the unofficial end of the **Viking Age.**

1200	The first Icelandic **sagas** are written.
1350	The Norse population on Greenland begins to decrease.
1408	A wedding takes place at Hvalsey Church on Greenland. It is the last Norse event to be recorded there.
1492	Christopher Columbus sails west from Spain and "discovers" America, not knowing that Vikings had traveled there almost 500 years earlier.
1721	A **Protestant missionary** comes to Greenland to convert the Greenlanders. He finds no Norse, only **Inuit.**
1898	A farmer in Minnesota discovers what he claimed to be a Norse runestone. It is most likely a fake.
1961	Helge Ingstad discovers Leif's camp at L'Anse aux Meadows.

More Books to Read

Craig, Claire. *Explorers & Traders*. Alexandria, Va.: Time-Life, Incorporated, 1999.

Osborne, Mary Pope. *Favorite Norse Myths*. New York: Scholastic, Inc., 2001.

Rees, Rosemary. *The Vikings*. Chicago: Heinemann Library, 2002.

Glossary

Althing name of the government assembly in Iceland

ancestor relative from the distant past

archaeologist scientist who studies ancient people by examining the items they left behind

artifact common item left behind by a group of people

banished forced out of a country after committing a crime

bishop religious leader in some Christian faiths

Byzantium ancient empire centered in what is now Turkey

caribou type of deer with large antlers; also called reindeer

colony group of people sent out by a state or country to settle a new territory

cove small bay or inlet

descendant child, grandchild, or other distant relative of a person or group of people

Dorset native people of Greenland during the 10th century

expedition trip taken to discover land or conduct trade

fjord narrow part of the sea between cliffs or steep slopes

futhark name of the runic alphabet used by the Vikings

glacier large mass of ice and snow that moves very slowly

Inuit Native American from Alaska who settled in northern Canada and Greenland

keel main body of a ship

knorr Viking ship used to carry cargo and people

landnam Scandinavian word meaning "land-taking," or settling on newly found land

longship Viking ship used for battle, often decorated with a dragon on the prow

missionary person who tries to convince others to accept a new religion

monastery place where monks live and pray

monk member of a religious group that lives apart from ordinary society

nautical relating to the sea and sailing

navigate to find the right direction during a journey

New World name given by Europeans to lands now known as South, Central, and North America

Norman Viking who settled primarily in northern France

Norse people originally from Norway who settled Iceland and Greenland

Protestant follower of a type of Christianity that developed to protest certain teachings of the Roman Catholic Church

prow front tip of a ship

Roman Catholic Church Christian faith led by the pope in Rome

runes system of writing used by the Vikings

saga book written in Iceland containing history and fables

Scandinavia European countries of Denmark, Norway, and Sweden; sometimes also includes Finland and Iceland

skirmish small, quick battle

skraeling Norse term for the native people of North America

styri Scandinavian word for a special oar used to steer a ship; led to the English word "starboard," the right side of a ship

tapestry piece of art woven from yarn and hung on a wall

Viking name given to people from Scandinavia who raided and then settled in western Europe and Russia between 750 and 1050

Western Hemisphere half of the world that includes North and South America and surrounding waters

Index